D1285897

DISCARDED:

OUTDATED, REDUNDANT
MATERIAL

Date: 8/18/16

BR 599.657 HAN
Hansen, Grace,
Moose /

PALM BEACH COUNTY
LIBRARY SYSTEM
3650 SUMMIT BLVD.
WEST PALM BEACH, FL 33406

Moose

by Grace Hansen

Abdo
ANIMALS OF
NORTH AMERICA
Kids

abdopublishing.com

Published by Abdo Kids, a division of ABDO, PO Box 398166, Minneapolis, Minnesota 55439.

Copyright © 2016 by Abdo Consulting Group, Inc. International copyrights reserved in all countries. No part of this book may be reproduced in any form without written permission from the publisher.

Printed in the United States of America, North Mankato, Minnesota.

102015

012016

 THIS BOOK CONTAINS RECYCLED MATERIALS

Photo Credits: iStock, Shutterstock

Production Contributors: Teddy Borth, Jennie Forsberg, Grace Hansen

Design Contributors: Laura Mitchell, Dorothy Toth

Library of Congress Control Number: 2015941759

Cataloging-in-Publication Data

Hansen, Grace.

 Moose / Grace Hansen.

   p. cm. -- (Animals of North America)

ISBN 978-1-68080-112-5 (lib. bdg.)

Includes index.

1. Moose--Juvenile literature.   I. Title.

599.65/7--dc23

                          2015941759

Table of Contents

Moose

Moose are found in the northern United States. They also live in Canada, Europe, and Asia.

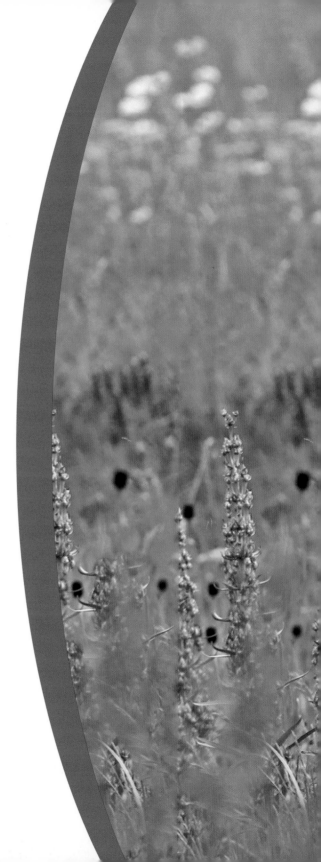

Moose live in forested areas. They live near lakes and streams. They cool off in the water on hot summer days. Their homes get snow in winter.

Moose are brown. They are very big. They have long legs and large bodies.

9

Moose have large hooves.

Their hooves help them

move over snow.

Male moose have antlers.
They use their antlers to
fight one another. They
shed their antlers each winter.

13

Food & Eating

Moose spend most of their
time eating. It is hard for
them to get low to the ground.
They search for food higher up.

15

Moose like to eat leaves, bark, and other plant parts. Moose are good swimmers. So they also eat lots of water plants.

Baby Moose

Baby moose are called calves. Calves are born in spring. Mothers usually have 1 or 2 calves.

19

Calves weigh about 30 pounds (13.6 kg) at birth. They grow fast. They can run when they are five days old!

21

More Facts

- Moose are the largest of the deer species.

- Moose eat pinecones. They are crunchy treats!

- Though they are big, moose can run up to 35 miles per hour (56 km/h).

Glossary

hooves – the special hard coverings on the feet of some animals.

shed – to lose as part of a natural process of life.

Index

abdokids.com

Use this code to log on to abdokids.com and access crafts, games, videos, and more!

Abdo Kids Code:

AMK1125